UNSPOKEN

Unwavering Honesty... Poems And Short Stories

Sherring Hope

Amazon Book Publishing Center 420 Terry Ave N, Seattle, Washington, 98109, U.S.A

The opinions expressed by the Author are not necessarily those held by Amazon Book Publishing Center.

Amazon Book Publishing Center works with authors, and aspiring authors, who have a story to tell and a brand to build.
Do you have a book idea you
would like us to consider publishing?

Please visit amazonbookpublishingcenter. com
for more information.

Dedication:

This book shall be my legacy. Proof that I lived, cried, laughed, hurt and loved here in this world. I dedicate it to my Daughter, my family, my twin grandsons and My friends.

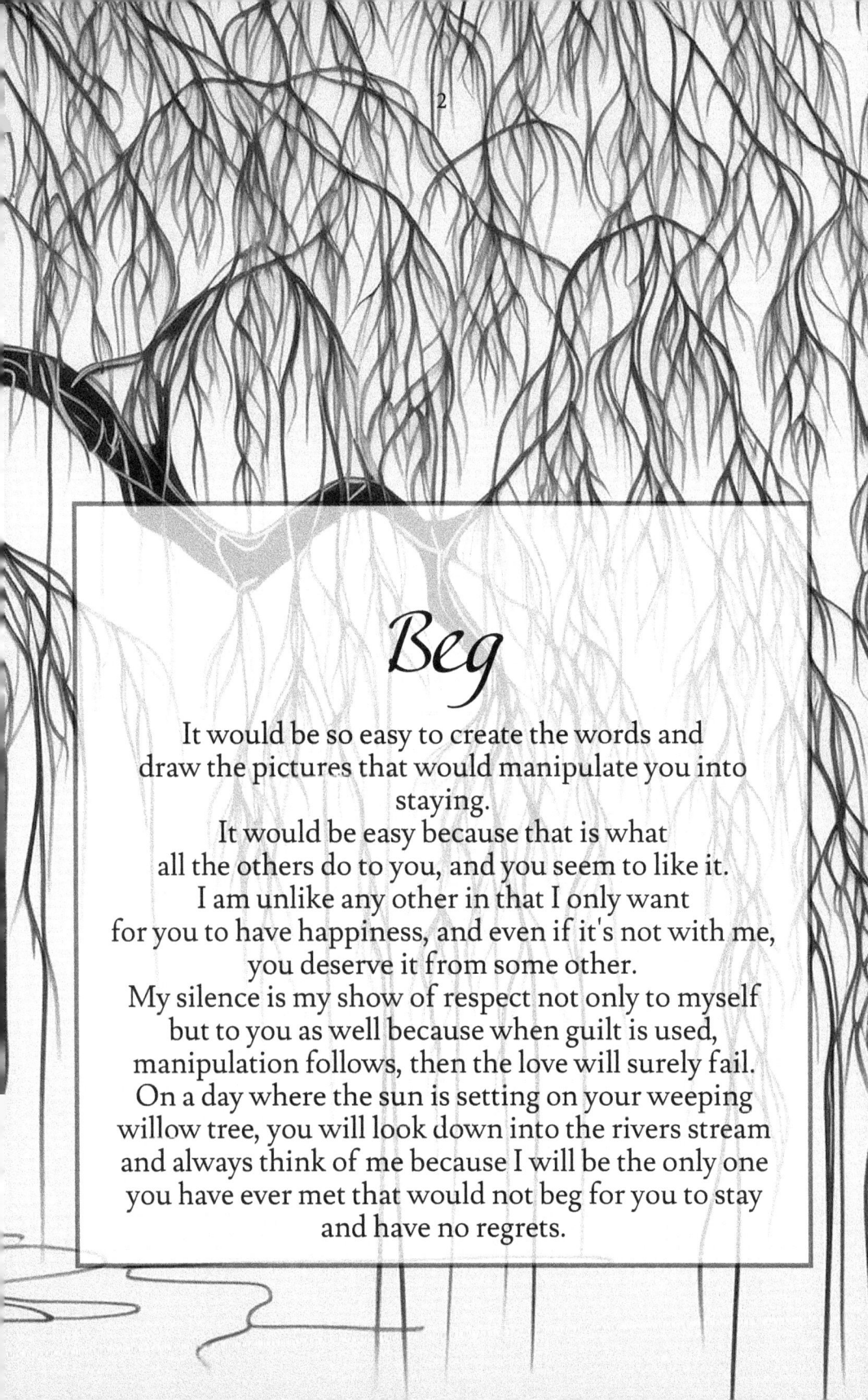

Beg

It would be so easy to create the words and
draw the pictures that would manipulate you into
staying.
It would be easy because that is what
all the others do to you, and you seem to like it.
I am unlike any other in that I only want
for you to have happiness, and even if it's not with me,
you deserve it from some other.
My silence is my show of respect not only to myself
but to you as well because when guilt is used,
manipulation follows, then the love will surely fail.
On a day where the sun is setting on your weeping
willow tree, you will look down into the rivers stream
and always think of me because I will be the only one
you have ever met that would not beg for you to stay
and have no regrets.

Your Soul People

Not everyone will speak fluent you
Not everyone has a mind and heart so true
People will always come into your life
but won't always be able to say
There are some however that would never
dream of ever going away
You couldn't loose them even if you tried
Your people know you inside and out as if you are an
extension of their own personal pride
Your people always come to your side even if you need
them from a distance whether
you are happy or while you cry
You would do anything for
each other yes even lie for instance
These are your soul people and they will always love you
and always be with you throughout your life
Rare people who travel through life together
and stand by each other through any kind
of weather are truly your
Best friends

Can't

I can't see you as clearly
now when I close my eyes anymore
It's harder to recognize your face
when it's not behind the mask you wore
Once your softly whispered words
felt like a gentle caress on my neck
Now the softer you speak,
I hear the demons in your
head with their plans and regrets
I don't see any kind of future now
beyond the haunting mountain of goodbyes
I can't love you and also be unscathed by the lies
My childhood self never dreamt love
would ruin and scar in this way.
I can't go on carrying
your baggage on my back because
I have my own filled with
demons to unpack and throw away.
Please walk away now and know in some way
that you won, be happy
for yourself and move on.
Let me off of this ride. I can't. I'm done
I can't live in your amusement park anymore
I just can't you won

No words

Silence consumes my thoughts
Answer my whys and why nots
Clarity arrives on sanities wings
Listen as she sings
Peace comes from within the soul
Minds have no reason to be told
Words have no true meaning from lips of a sinner
They swirl and twirl and confuse your reasoning
Where truth is lacking, words become blurred
Listen to your wisdom from within.
They are your words
Silence can sometimes be your only true friend
Learn to listen to it.
It will lead you within

Us

I am wiser now. I lived a life of stupidity, and
hard lessons learned that left scars, and yes,
surprisingly, they still do sometimes burn.
I see in your soul it turns in turmoil the same as mine but
in a different time, endless pondering and thrusted hate
that leached on to me not wanting to ever let go.
My eyes fixate. They see in yours what once was in mine.
My darkest regrets and tears
fill all the chests of hope that end this time.
Destiny intertwines our souls, giving me a symbol of hope
to renew faith in the future I once held dear and helping
you find growth from my pains to learn your precious
worth to learn you are all that you ever will need and that
life is ever-changing and vast in just a moment...
years pass.
I wish you could grow from my pain instead of feeling
your own heal from my lessons and move on.
I wish for you...
Never let go of your beautiful soul.

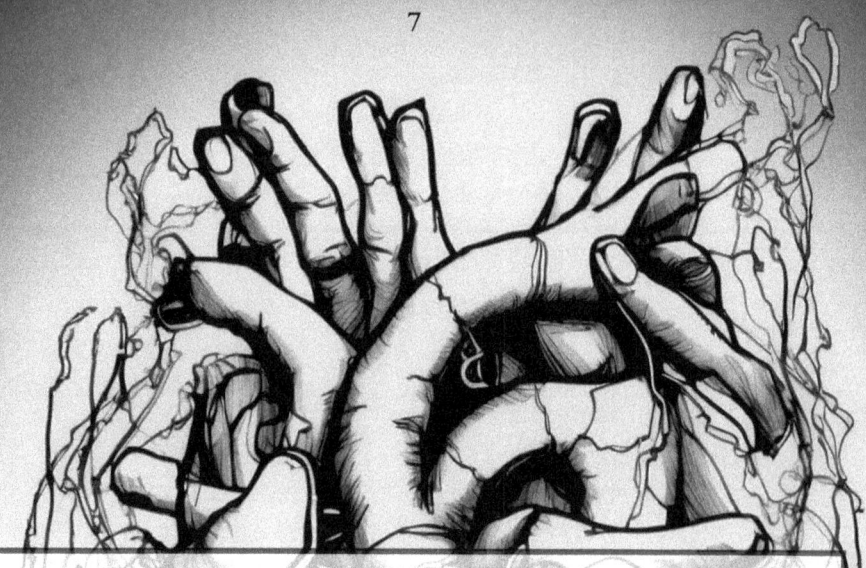

Only for yourself

If you truly cared, you'd walk
away and leave me be here to figure out my way.
Here where I have fought, cried and
drowned in sorrow and felt my heart break.
If I was the one your only desire
You'd want only for me to figure out
how to move out of your fire
You want only for you
You don't care who you screw
Your intentions are to consume the depths of my soul
Keep me captive until my heart is dead and cold
If you truly cared, you'd want
only to see me fly again, fly again, and so far away from
you where I might heal and begin.
But you don't care for anyone unless it serves your
needs, so full of consumption and literal destruction as
long as you win.

Beautiful

Unused beautiful piece of paper on
which I make my memories on
Moments of disgrace used up with holes left
where words were erased
Torn all into pieces and thrown away
Is this life now over
Reaching in and pulling out the discarded pieces
finding their place one by one
The paper is reassembled but never the same.
Once unused, it is now wrinkled and scarred
where the lines connect, putting the pieces back
just like my heart.
Beautifully sewn paper from so long ago
has more memories than you'd ever know.

My song

The darkest pools of invigorating life
reflecting wanting deepest desires
When I look into those eyes
Sensual excitement and sinful suggestions
fly from those incredible lips, so sexual
When I see that grinning smile
mischievous and craving life, inviting me in just
lights my fire burning within
When I hear that laugh
Comforting and beautiful, broken
but wanting so much more happily ever after
When I feel the connection between my soul and yours
Urning anticipation sparks a flame
When you play that song on my heartstrings

Flooded

I lost you once some time ago, and your face
had started to fade; you haunted me as a ghost.
Letting you go was never my intention as you were
amongst one of my favorite life treasures
I loved and cherished the most..
A heavy price for it, I dearly did
pay, day after endless days.
Little did I know then I'd never feel
again about anything quite that same way
Shadows suddenly move out of the darkness into the
light as I stand still in the moving
time a vision colorful and vivid your
face appears again in my sight.
A regret no more; we were meant for this life.
Never again shall I lose this lightening never
strikes twice, not in the same place
Filled with peace, happiness and love
So happy you are in my life;
my emotions are flooded

Hush

Hush, little darling dry your eyes
The thoughts in your
head are making you cry
Wipe away those tears and give a big sigh
And Sing yourself a happy little lullaby
Go to sleep now. Have sweet dreams
When you wake up in the morning,
you'll feel new things

Smile

The feeling that finds you when you least expect it
The one that brings on the brightest
and unforgettable moments
Your hair stands up, and butterflies
are under attack in your stomach
It's a feeling you will never ever forget
Your grinning smile does these things to me
Makes me feel things I just can't believe
And with one look, I'm down on my knees
Smile again for me smile again, please
It is then that fate reminds me that
I can still have everything I need

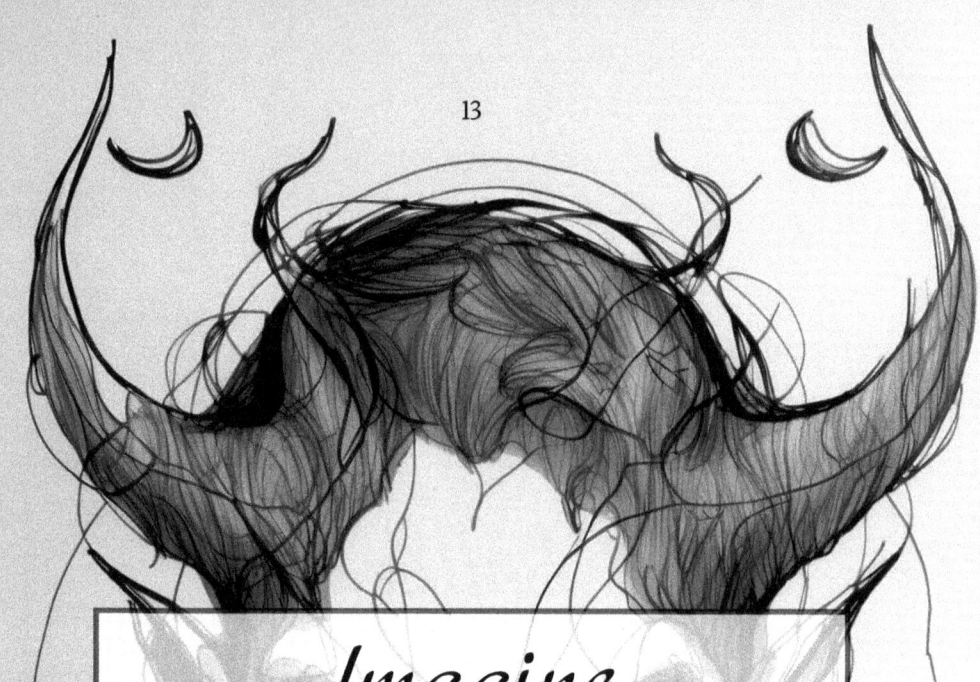

Imagine

He has darkness. He has demons
It lurks deep down inside him
Kept hidden away, there are secrets and lies
waiting to destroy anyone that gets inside
It means to strip you down raw
and degrade you make you cry
His darkness wears many faces,
humiliates and misleads you
It wants to own you, punish you
deface and disgrace you
He trains it to capture your spirit
and to imagine a life all consuming within it
He has darkness, and it means to
destroy you with insidious intent
Pay close attention, and you won't
get captured by it again protect your
heart smartly, and you will win at
this game called life just
Imagine

Blurred

Clear mind with pure heart, I can
no longer tell the lines apart
I was standing over there, but now
I am over here
How do I know which side to take cause
now I don't see a way that is clear
Something's changed the
direction in which my heart beats
Never thought I'd be in this situation again.
I guess I am just weak
It's a different type of yearning,
a purely satisfying feeling
Something you want but can't explain
I feel like I am bringing on my own pain
I'm in too deep now. How did this happen
How did I let it get so far
How do I navigate this without leaving scars
How do I know if the feeling is the same
Is it written in the stars
Help me navigate these blurred lines
Please help me to see everything to avoid the pain

Pushing it down

Pushing it all down, but eventually,
it will overfill, explode and work its way back up.
Express yourself now or deal with it again later.
Only you are being hurt by your
obvious attempts at denial.
The heart wants what it wants,
and sooner or later, it won't be ignored.
You think you have it all under control
by simply closing the door.
If you don't address the truth now,
all those bottled up things you
have been ignoring will come bursting
through that closed door but
be even stronger than before
Stop running away and settle the score

Carry

I carry your memories around with me,
etched in my mind and burned into my soul.
Try as I might, they don't get
replaced with new ones as I grow old
So you may still hold a place deep down inside me
But that place is an empty space,
a stain that shames and reminds me that once
I put it all out there just to
have it come back to me all broken,
and I don't even recognize it covered
in the lies that you've sewn and spoken.
I carry you with me, but now you serve as a painful
memory to be aware of the people who serve
themselves first. They are the ones who never
truly care and will defile you while
quenching their own thirst.
No one said life was fair.

Everlasting

Profanity murders eloquently
Darkness consumes blindlessly
Painful captures artfully
Careless cripples wholeheartedly
Longing crushes hopefully
Untrusting leaves disparity
Passionless attracts complacently
Unworthy manifests possibility
Everlasting... doubtfully

Promises

Trust me, rolls off your tongue like water
down a river headed straight for the falls.
Demons peer from behind the blackness in your eyes,
a careless sinner with sinister lies.
Blacken heart is made of pure evil,
and you can not hide the hate you curate inside,
intent on manipulating with hurtful disguises.
I thought you loved me once but found out the hard way
that love for you is not the same
in the hell you were created from
Promises from you are like drowning
in my own blood pool. I'm not a muse or your fool.
Unraveling in your hands is the life I take
back before you kill my soul with your empty
promises and devastating contempt.

It's Time

It's time for me to finally let you go now.
To stop wondering about the what
ifs and all the some how's
Holding on to the things I thought it was,
but they really never were
My heart was certain, but yours was never sure.
It's all starting to fade and blur.
And honestly, the truth is that it's done and over,
and none of it even matters anymore.
I lost the trust I once had in my gut abilities,
but even still, as I conjure this confession, I can't help
but think of you and how you knew I was yours.
I guess I was blindly eager to see only
what you wanted me to believe.
I know I asked you to go, but I waited in standing time
for you to put up a fight, but instead, you slipped away
unsettling quietly, and now I know I wasn't right.
So it's time for me to let this go and set myself
free and hope that one day, very soon that,
I'll see who you really never were to me.

Peace

How can there be peace while
I'm living in tattered pieces
Astonished by your deceit
Creeping around town
Wearing disguises like a clown
Carefully planting lies
Spreading spew like a demon
You vile venomous snake
Which face is the fake
Cut you down piece by piece
Rebuilding my devastated soul
Until my heart is at peace and whole

Awaken

Pilfered looted, dazed and confused
My soul was closed years ago for misuse
When out of the blue, your tears caught my eye
In your voice, I heard my own cries
I've been awakened
Desperate to share with you
The damage years of abuse will do
Feverishly jotting down
Jumbled up random memories
frightening how my words just pour out.
It's how my heart screams and shouts
It's your weary soul that called to me
Desperate and disparaging pleas
Its time to awaken wanting to help spare you pain
I jump right in fight the fight
because our souls are eerily the same

Grief

Tarnished glances and a painted-on smile
Lurking in corners while trying to hide
Haunting voices penetrate my defenses
Promises handed out like candy alerts my senses
What lies behind that devilish stare that
makes my hair stand up in the air
Master game player reveals his setlist.
Who will prevail as a champion of my world
while it's set on fire and filled with turmoil?
Exhaustion defeats the feelings that are all there.
The final blows will be devastating and cause me despair.
Dawn arrives she begins to
clear the sky of the darkened gray night
Brings hope of something new on a beautiful day while
learning to grieve for losses that weren't meant to stay
End of my story has yet to be written
Only myself is declared my own winner

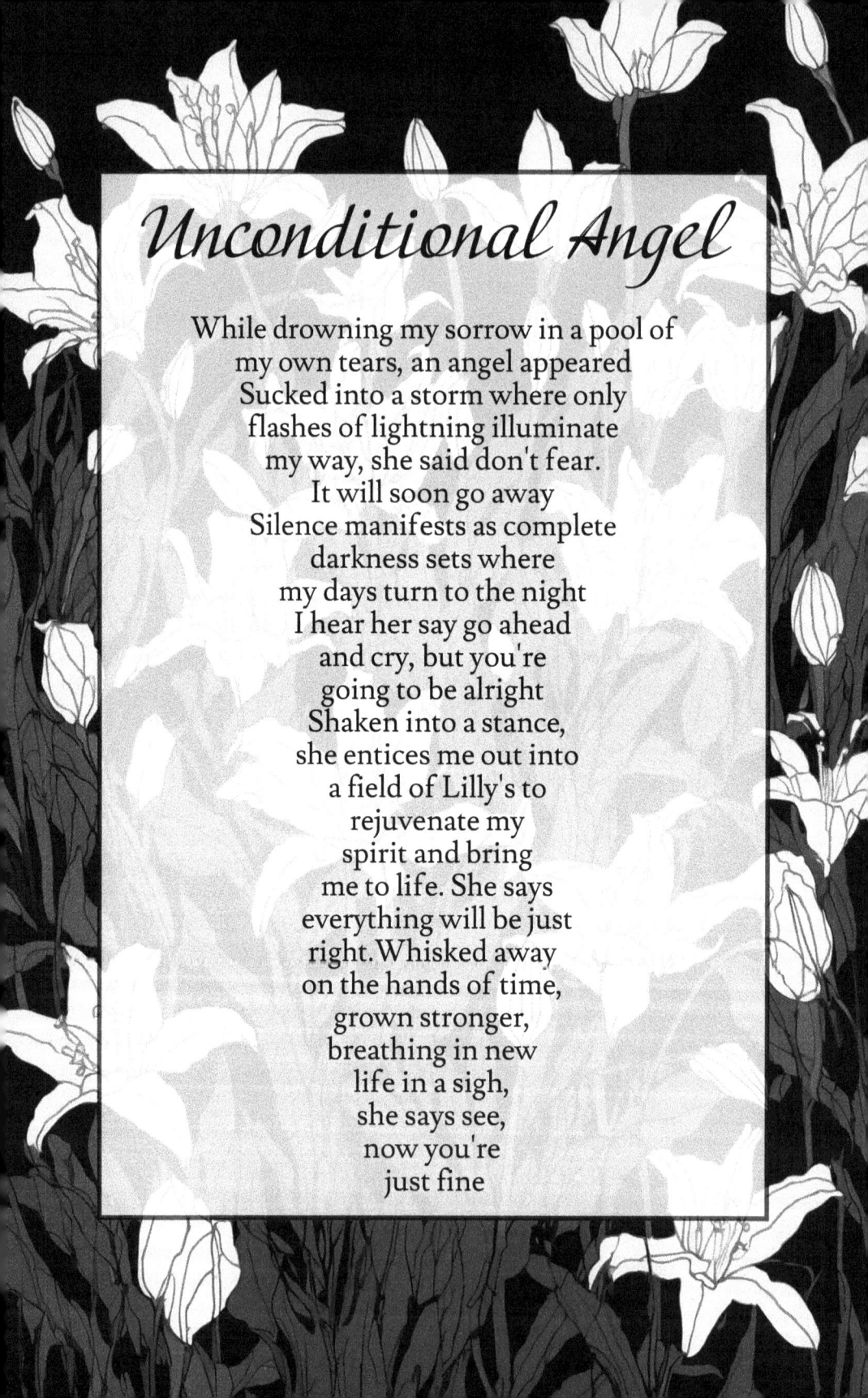

Unconditional Angel

While drowning my sorrow in a pool of
my own tears, an angel appeared
Sucked into a storm where only
flashes of lightning illuminate
my way, she said don't fear.
It will soon go away
Silence manifests as complete
darkness sets where
my days turn to the night
I hear her say go ahead
and cry, but you're
going to be alright
Shaken into a stance,
she entices me out into
a field of Lilly's to
rejuvenate my
spirit and bring
me to life. She says
everything will be just
right. Whisked away
on the hands of time,
grown stronger,
breathing in new
life in a sigh,
she says see,
now you're
just fine

Insane

I'd never have thought it
I swear, not even for a minute
I can't believe just how well you hid it
Empty words leave your lips
Shameless eyes disguise your intent
Just a shell of a coward
You have no soul, so misleading
Leaving a path of destruction and bleeding
The only person you love is insane
The devil sat down beside me today
The two began a dance to see who will win the
game neither knew the rules, and both were only insane.

Deafening

Deafening darkness blankets my sight
Repetitious scenarios plaque my mind
Insidious intent blackens my soul
heartache ensues by puncturing blows
Shattered, fractured pieces are scattered
Crawling wavering stumbling patterns
Forsaken banished irrelevant matters
Illuminate emancipate nurturing saddens
Salvation replenish the beautiful you
Life again, deafening light

Don't

Don't say what you think I want to hear
Because of that reason is why I write this in tears
If you truly loved me,
nothing could've torn you away
Nothing in the world could've
made you lie and manipulate me this way
I won't ever hate you, but in my heart, I now
know there can never be
a place for you to roam freely
Never again will you darken
my soul with hate and disgrace
Never again will you lie to my face
The trust is gone it's far too late
Don't say words you think will change my mind
because I have grown wise beyond your kind.
Time for you to go now... don't say a word
None of them matter
Don't.... they hurt

Sober

Sober and dry
Recovering clean
from intoxicating lies
Masquerading disguise
Meaningless dreams
Didn't mean a thing
Fraudulent truths
Incriminating proof
forcing events
Downward spiral
Mind-bending viral
Insane mentally unstable
You'll pay someday
Suffering dismay
Never be able
To stay sober

Your Devil

Your devil that lurks inside you
broke free and walked beside you just a
little while for all the world to see
Your ability to be Deceitfully charming was
really quite alarming, but now
everyone has seen your true face
underneath your true identity.
How could I miss the manipulating
ways you'd make a fool out of me?
Your cocky little devil played the game too
long and found out just
how strong and cunning I could be
Take your pretty words and all your seductive
lies and go straight back to hell,
you evil devil in disguise
You no longer have power over me

Watching

Standing there in this
never-ending circle defined by your life
You are watching all
the years that have gone on by
You reach out to catch
a moment, but it moves in haste
The circle keeps repeating
there's just no more time to waste
You see it all happening and
know the cycle has to come to an end
You'll certainly have another
broken heart ceremony to attend
Where trust once was now
just a moment fleeting by
Why can't you finally break
this circle and choose to change your life
You will regret it if you don't do it fast
because life happens in flashes as it flies past
While you stand there
watching, wondering why didn't I?
You've lost several
moments once more of a good life.

So now what

Hold onto hope or let the possibility of it go
How do I fill the void of a defeated, empty soul
everything you ever promised me
Everything you made me believe
Is this one of those life's little lessons
that is supposed to teach me, yet
How devastatingly cruel can this life truly be
now when I open my eyes on a gloriously beautiful
morning, I see straight through where your presence was,
and morning turns to mourning.
When do the tears all dry up and turn to sparkles that
glow? So now what and where do I go
My mind is screaming, but you can't see my heart breaking
All my friends think it's for the best
just suck it up you were mistaken
Where do I find the courage to accept what I
won't ever know, and how do I trust whose
hand to hold and who's to let go
who will help me to heal and to grow
So now what help me take back my soul

Deceit

Undying admiration
Created in deceit
You lied while I believed
now I cry while you retreat
Shameless cruelty defines your intentions
Bleed me dry of all my sentiments
Steal from me my everything
Drowning in disbelief and sorrow
I will pick myself back up
and move on somehow tomorrow
Innocence buried with insidious deceit

Shattered

I wish I could go back before my world shattered
I'd pick and choose the things that mattered
I'd make our last memory one you'd never ever forget
I'd call you out on the games and bullshit
I'd take away your manipulative power
Crush your lies and make you go cower
I wish I could go back before I shattered
I could stop what was put into motion
Take back the time that you've wrongfully stolen
If I could put back the pieces that shattered,
I'd pick and choose only the ones that mattered.
None of them would
include you getting the best of me
All of them would be
of me being set free un shattered

Damaged

Surrounded in moments fleeting
Denying me the air I'm breathing
Scratching, clawing, desperately needing
Organs slowly dying and bleeding
Seeping out onto the earth beneath me
Soulless-stained, cowardly cheating
Ruiner depletes artfully deceiving
Bestow mischievous, carefully misleading
Retreat, revive, saving save my life
Fire flames eternally mystified
Won't be taken in again by lies

Caretaker

Were you put here to help
me heal and save my life,
or was I put here to
help you find your strength to fight
I've never met anyone more like me than myself
Not quite sure how this came about
You were present when I was young
I wrote you instructions in a poem
dated years before you were born
I explain to you how to move on and
let go from my experiences all those years ago.
Then we have music, art, poetry and laughter,
trauma empathy, cats and disasters
Abuse recluse sadness and hurt
abandonment, regrets, jokes and jerks
So much laughter these things
and so much more form a
bond that linked our souls
Yours is newer but feels much older
Mine is older but feels much younger
Our caretaker ways helped forge a
friendship for which I am thankful every day.

Pool of tears

Penetrating sadness burns as it deepens farther and
farther, and the light is dimming.
Return me my dignity and the dreams that once
filled my soul. You trespass now, leave the keys, just go.
Peering deep inside, nothing
is there where life once was and
Darkness seeps into the words that once
held you so far above the rest
Sorrow greedily drinks from
my growing pool of tears and jests
Leave me now as I muster up a stagger to retreat
and regain the ragged pieces of
me that you so carelessly scattered
My weary heart is no longer yours to drain

Storm

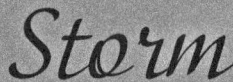

Dropped straight out of a tornado funnel
Covered in emotional debris and turmoil
Still chasing the storm, she smells of lightening
and thunder
With no idea where it will lead as she moves on
down the path chasing the storm
Emotional wreckage left behind was immense,
and the ending has not
ended but will prove to be severe and intense
Staggering pain from tasting the lightening is
causing her to self-destruct
while trying to find her footing in this life again
she tells herself she will be okay if she can just get
one more peek at the sunshine-wrapped rainbow
that is hidden in the darkness
and angry clouds of the tornado
The force is pulling it is just too much.
She has to give up and begin to rebuild again
Chasing the storm never ends

Better than you

While trying to be there for you
Care for you, educate you to save you
It became so clear to me
You brought me back to a place I fear
the most, a place where I once lost my soul.
Warning you of his lies
Caught yours in disguise
Unmasking his manipulations
Found myself in the same situation
Wasting time denying your instincts
Keeping you sane, I did the same thing
Seems as though while trying to save you
from yourself, I went and lost me again.
I'm no better than you.

Dignity

Desecration of my dignity
Flailing about, trying to catch my breath
Words fail me as I fall to the ground
The earth is unforgiving under my breasts, my body
protected by dampened, moist leaves.
The air smells of my shame. I detest time to retreat
Help me shed this steel chain that
binds me to my sorrowful tears
Frightened by a juvenile soul
filled with remorse and fears
Has it begun? Yes, my story painfully unfolds
But the ending is still unknown.
It remains unwritten unsoiled untold
Hope lingers as my heart mends
There's still time to begin yet again
Time heals all wounds in the end
So they say don't let them take
your dignity away... again

Night Sky

Billowing arrogant clouds give shape
to the massive night skies backdrop.
Inspiring wonder and ushering
in a familiar cool breeze
The moon struggles to hang and
glow as the painted sunset silently kneels.
This summer's passing left traces of an unfulfilled
need that sparked a burning desire in me.
Winter barrels in with fresh, brisk air and a new
outlook on what could be instead of what could've been
Blankets so soft music inspiring laughter and
unforgettable moments and where bonfires
invite new people and memories to begin
But none of these things will occur with the greatest
of ease as my mind is frozen in time back to a place
where the summer night sky was host to warm, steamy
feelings and I could still touch your face,
and so there is where we will always be in my
most treasured memories kept safe.
Unforgettable moments made against the night sky

Left Behind

Tapestries, stories,
sculptures is there time to capture
and love the things we
want to have and cherish
Canvas colors are vivid and dark
there will be an etched
portrait of your smile on my heart.
Charcoal and ink expressively display
Words from my heart,
ones I didn't and can't say
I'll travel on down this road for a while
and wear your memories
like a badge that will make me smile
we will laugh and talk about you to others we
meet along the way of all the good times
we've had and how you couldn't stay

Once Again

Weary soul searching for rejuvenation and hope
to search for new pieces to again make it whole.
Cleanse out the night terrors made up of all lies
and refill the heart with self-love and endless pride.
In this life, you weren't ever quite right
Behind that mask, darkness hides within
You've fallen on your tarnished sword again and again
Those deep holes left in all those you used
Will fill again with peace and happiness, life renewed.

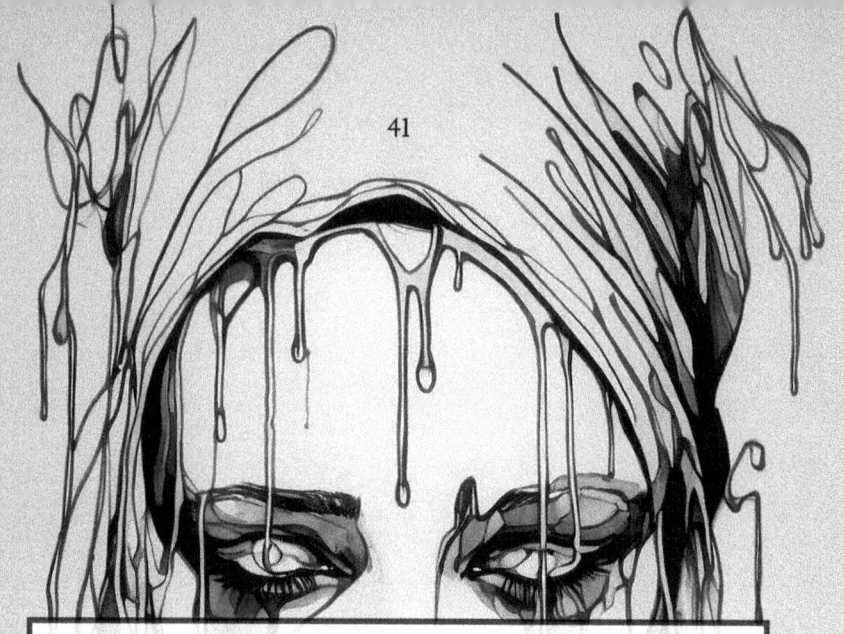

Cry

When she cries
You should feel her
raw staggering pain
When she cries
You should drown from
her tears in vain
As she cries
You should fall to your
knees on shards of broken glass
As she cries
You should beg her
forgiveness, but none
given backbecause she cries
Your cruelty no longer has a place to hide
Because she cries, you should
choke on your manipulative lies
Now you cry, go on and cry
Hope you remember the pain until you die
You imprinted on my soul

You

Trying to escape you, so I ran
I ran away to nowhere, but I still ran
I turn a corner but can see you there, so I ran
I run away to elude you, but I can't
Screwing with my head must excite you
So I run
Trying hard to hide from you, but I'm done
now I think I'll make my stand
you feel nothing inside you, and I still can
Let that be your eternal punishment
Watch me move on because I finally can

Nothing

How dare you return me my heart all
Tattered and torn
Your disparaging words unravel my last nerve.
Yeah, I see your horns
Sheer contempt swallows you whole
while the darkest sludge fills your soul
Determined to demolish all of my hopes
You dishonorably fall on your sword as demons
tighten the rope
Just walk away now. Please just go nothing left of
your handy work here, nothing left to trample on,
nothing left of you to fear
Nothing Just go

Easy Love

Once in your life, an easy feeling
takes hold and leads you home.
A love so kind and gentle but also raw and invigorating
Every day flows like an endless river cascading
Your urges are quieted, and you no longer need to roam
When someone breaks into your broken world and shows
you what a completed version of yourself looks like,
grab hold of them and hold on tight
This doesn't happen to many some never do at all
Easy love is the purest kind of love
Don't fight the fall

Broken

Woke up again today, and you weren't here.
Can't remember the last time I saw your face
next to mine in the bathroom mirror
The air in here is stale.
It reeks of cigarettes and beer
Reality mingles with my dreams in some dark
god-forsaken place. It's hard to tell
what's the truth and what is fake
I feel so faithless walking around
in a dazed and confused state of mind
Everything fell apart it's all broken now.
This will be our final goodbye slivers of my heart
sink to the bottom of the ocean no, not that one,
but the one made up of
all of my remorseful tears, so many that
they set the changing tides in motion
There's no turning back nothing left
of the love we had you had the best of me
Broken promises are all that's
left of these forever etched-in memories

Round

Merry go round
Escapes the ground
Swirling in the air
Jumping clown
Blood-curdling sounds
threatening glares
Fearfully bound
Crazy fiery hair
Round n round it goes
Get up, fall back down
Merry go round

Mummum

Would you look at those green meadows
I see green, but what is it?
Shaking hands with all the Greenbay Packers
Could you be any more excited
If I look a bit harder, it could be the Grinch
The two of you with those snide little grins
But still, it's so pretty and green, and the sun is setting
Have you ever seen anything so grey?
Wait? The horizon is actually heard
of grey elephants coming this way
You do love elephants, don't you?
Settle in with a book of crossword puzzles and
your fuzzy Cali cat. Sleep well. It's been a hard day.
Dream of family and keep them safe.

Silent Tears

**(I wrote in high school and won 1st place
in a state literary competition for short stories.)**

Out on the edge, a helpless child peers over the side. As he looks
down, he wonders if what's down there would be better for him.
His face is bruised, and his body is small. He hasn't slept or eaten for
days, he does not want to live at all.

You see, the boy has a cold and cannot control his cough. His
father, earlier, had sternly warned him he'd better stop coughing.
Involuntarily the cough burst out, and within a moment's time,
his father was in a rage and began his assault. Nothing could stand
in his way. The boy lay helpless under this big, powerful man. His
mother, in the kitchen, didn't hear a thing, nothing at all. She was
remembering back to their wedding day;
she looked at her ring.

When the beating ended, the hurting child, mindful of all the times
before and thinking this would not be the last, ran off behind a
church. There flowed a River full of old rain and newly fallen tears.

The boy stands and wonders: Isn't there anybody near to hear me
cry? Can't anybody help ease my pain?

But if he jumps, he will never hurt again.
With emotions wild and tears rolling down his face, he falls asleep.

When he awakens later that same evening, still looking over the river
and knowing that his father will kill him if he continues coughing,
he starts the walk back to his home.

Nearing the house, he notices his father pacing the floor. Chills run
through his body. As he walks onto the front porch, he hesitates, and
the fear of his father turns him back to the river. There he can find
the peace he's been searching for. As night and day become one, the
river consumes his body and the last of his tears.

Touch

Can I touch you there
Is there enough of you to share
Will you unlock your door
Can't take the anticipation anymore
Can I kiss you there where you glisten
You'd have to relinquish control
You'd find me wandering bare
Lingering teasing caressing you there,
spreading ecstasy, there's no compare
Your sighs of oh-so-much pleasure
Your moans of release, I treasure
means the absolute most to me
Can I touch you there, pretty, please
Soothing and growing your soul
I don't ever want to leave
Can I touch you there in your soul

Flowing

Open heartedly and brutally honest
from the depths of the soul.
Words force their way out like a lightening bolt from the
sky, beautiful and bold
Just like lyrics to music, free to be whatever they will be,
someone's story is born or ending and needs to be told.
Mindlessly flowing, they bind together
to make sense of tangled up feelings.
Writing the things you don't or
can't always say sets you free
Like a sunset pastel lights bursting through the clouds,
these words burst their way out
and settle onto a page with ease.
The things we wanna say flowing free

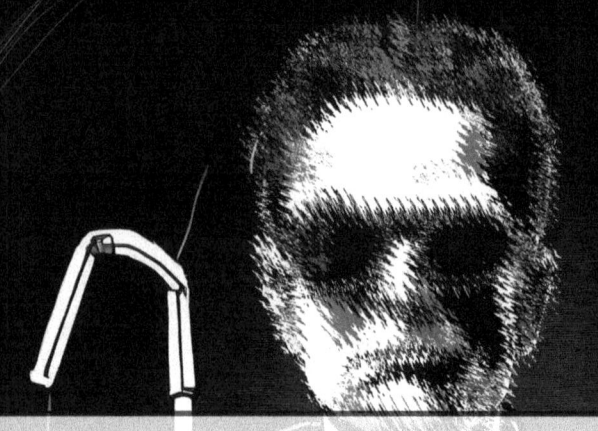

Soul raper

You forced your way in
with a slimy smile and sinister grin
Immediately calculating malicious intent
Studied in disquisition everything about
me
You did your due diligence.
Now it's time to defile me
head over heels for someone who lied to
me.
Who was this person I let deep inside
My soul was bare, my heart open wide
With blinders on, I had no way of knowing
False claims of who you really were to me
Same as being raped by a stranger, don't
you see? Kept your intent and truth well
hidden
A tragedy indeed is a soul raper
set free to bring hurt and
despair to the unsuspecting.

Goodbye

In every sense of the word a goodbye
feels irrevocably permanent
You were once here but gone in an instant
a memory in a fleeting moment
It lingers on you and in you
everywhere forcing memories causing despair
You feel it on your skin where a touch once
caressed you or ran through your hair
your lips moist once from a kiss
but now from tears falling like a rainy mist
Ripping through your soul leaving questions and regrets
your heart hurts with burning intense pain and is where
goodbye leaves the biggest scar yet by far a stain
Especially when goodbye came with no notice at all,
sometimes not even words were spoken
and it tears you all apart
Feeling empty and broken

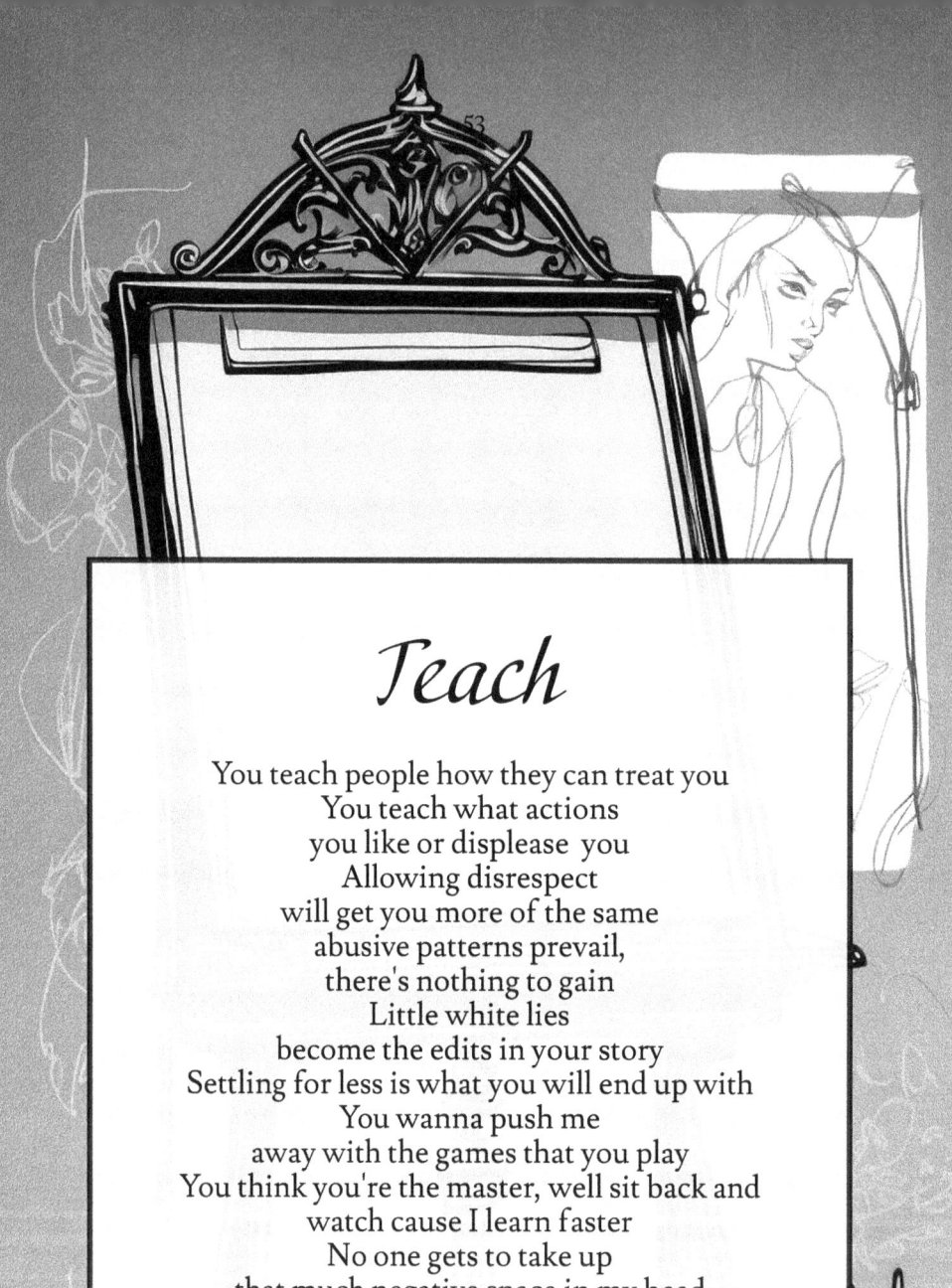

Teach

You teach people how they can treat you
You teach what actions
you like or displease you
Allowing disrespect
will get you more of the same
abusive patterns prevail,
there's nothing to gain
Little white lies
become the edits in your story
Settling for less is what you will end up with
You wanna push me
away with the games that you play
You think you're the master, well sit back and
watch cause I learn faster
No one gets to take up
that much negative space in my head
I won't play but be gone by morning instead
Head games are hurtful disguises to
manipulate the outcome of all the lies.
Teach me, hurt me,
treat me like I don't matter
I promise when I leave,
I'll be gone like none of this ever happened

Aching

Darkness devours translucent light
Penetrating every fracture of the soul
Morbid illusions creep into sanity creating deafening
visions of what's yet to behold
Despair bestows an abundance of masterful profanity
which massacres all hope of navigating soundly
Bleeding profusely, life drains
into the all-consuming earth
Colorful blindness silences
crying voices yearning to be heard
Stained shrouds of shame suffocating and smothering
Tattered and tainted, coveting one last glorious breath
Retreat to this crypt to lie down in the darkness
aching to find peace and comforting rest
here lies desecration. I have no more regrets.

You Haunt Me

Daybreak reveals the
games that were played.
You'll never be satisfied
with me as the winner,
not as long as your the perfect sinner
You haunt me deep down inside
it was your personal mission to try
To ruin my soul with
your malicious intentions
You took all of me away
There's nothing left to say
Nothing is okay
I put you in your place
You haunt me every day
How can you walk around insane
You lost, and I'm to blame
That's okay to say I'll say it every day
You have no shame. You are to blame
Go haunt someone else. Go away

Brutally Honest

I appreciate people who are brutally honest.
Only when I come across these rare souls do I choose to
share words over silence a true friendship unfolds
Genuine honesty over everything else
that is forced and easily faked
Conversations are riveting and intellectually exciting.
Trust flows freely because you are no longer hiding.
Honesty does not come easy for the faint
of heart who are used to lying.
Life makes it too easy to wear disguises,
hiding under a cloak denying.
I'd rather sit in silence with myself than have
mindless babble with someone who surmises
and lives their life as an unidentifiable ghost.

Games of the heart

Some you win, but most you lose when
games of the heart are what you choose
Carefully curated words or
knowing when to say nothing
Calculated moments devised
when taking the risk in trusting
Just when to hold on a little bit tighter
when you feel them starting to pull away
All ways in which people want to play
When is the right time to sacrifice your heart
Will it just end up torn all apart
Who wins and who ends up hurt
Games of the heart are for cowards
Don't play, take back your power
Someone always ends up hurt

Angel

Today another angel appeared and opened his mouth.
I know I have heard these words, the ones he spoke about
insightful and caring, his message was clear
As much as it hurt me, I needed to hear
Everything happens for a reason,
and I'm not fully to blame
Some of the angel swords peeled
back the layers, and I felt the pain
These angels seemingly need
to constantly reassure
and remind me
No one else
in this world can be
crueler to me
than I can be to
my own self, no-one
is perfect,
everyone needs a
little help,
we begin picking me up,
and I dust off
past mistakes
Little worse for the wear,
but this does not seal my fate
might have cried a few more tears this time,
but that knife was buried deep inside
Each time I attend one of my own heartbreaking events,
I'm sure this one will be the last on my end
It's up to me now to evaluate my harmful patterns.
I see them there, red and scattered
Learn from these lessons made of glass
and make the next time better than the last
As cruel as you can be to yourself, it also goes
that NO-ONE will ever love you more than
you respect and love yourself
Angel is wise and bares the scars of experience

Disturbances

When you became part of the disturbances
dancing in my head, then it's time for you to go
that stupid girl in me is dead.
No self-respecting demon would drag me
through that unfathomable pain again that's the
definition of insanity and regret locked in
They say with age comes wisdom they're the
dumbest of all wisdom only comes from the
worst lessons learned after the falls.
My wisdom has no bounds. I have fallen so
many times pretty sure this is life number 9
I walk hurriedly through this world like there's
some important place that I am bound, but
really, upon closer look, you'll soon see I'm
being chased by the past indiscretions that
wanna tear open my scars and won't let me be
Every chance they get, they've stolen pieces of
my soul, my dignity and self-respect, then a
voice of sound mind hits me over the head and
begs I remember my life lessons and that I fight
to take my shit back time to live my life.
Wisdom only comes with age if you don't
repeat the same mistakes.

Colors

You'll come across a chameleon
in life every now and then.
They are good at playing games
and changing their identity to fit in.
It is hard to spot these players are skilled
with full intent to win.
Not all of them are malicious.
Some have nothing but good intentions.
Searching for a place within them
that feels like home, warm and safe
But you will never really know which of the two you
have found or when their colors will change again, for if
something better comes along and gets too close, this new
colorful thing could eventually take your place.

My

Illusions manifested into memories
Memories clouded by deceit
How can I be strong when my heart feels defeat
Breaking through the soil, climbing into the light
Running so fast to escape my darkest of nights
Despair catches up as I struggle to catch my breath
Opens my wounds until there is nothing left
Fighting the fight called on by my own wits to sort
through this madness bit by bit, becoming so clear
that there's no sound defense
You came for me with malicious intent
Save my broken soul. I won't be ruined again.

Hole

Chained by my heart to
Walls of lies and pain
Eating from the scraps you
choose to throw me in vain
Ripping the skin, exposing the bone
I can't find my way clear of your torturous hold
Names faintly scattered of all those before
as I claw my way out of this deep dark hole.
Morning brings no comfort at all
The light hides there in the cracks
Throw down the rope and never return back
Survival kicks in, and I won't cower down
I plan to win

Never

No remorse, nothing left to say
Never thought you'd violate me this way
How did I miss the makings of your cruel intentions
Never saw that you were narrating the play
The devil curled up beside me
and declared his intent to stay and justify me.
His mask slipped a little but still covered his face
Making me his keeper unintended believer
I never could've fathomed his calculated ness
Don't whisper fake words of sorrow
He never felt a thing. Don't ask for my empathy because,
for you, that part of me is empty. Never speak to me again.
The feelings are dead
Never

Strangers

It's the strangest form of heartache when a person
you once cared so deeply for, filled every part of every day,
someone that you were completely happy with,
is just unexplainably gone in a day.
This person came into your life suddenly
like a lightning strike out of the bluest skies.
You fit together effortlessly,
and nothing before now had ever felt so right.
Silence became laughter,
and the Music played once again in your heart.
But while you were enjoying a piece of heaven,
they were searching for answers in a sea of
depthless souls off in their own inner dark.
What was a clear choice for you
had become only an option for them.
So now, with a heavy heart and weeping soul, you have
only one thing left to choose... let them go, make them go.
Let them waiver and falter on their own, and maybe one day,
they will find their way back to you like an old favorite song.
Choosing to stay silent when you have endless words to say takes
self discipline and is a show of respect not only to yourself but to
them as well because if persuasion is used, you'll always wonder
if they stayed for the right reasons
and if it's still only an impending option
for them to one day soon, regret
The scariest part of letting go, though, is you feel incomplete
with so much that was left unsaid and wondering if, during their
self discovering flight, they will miss
you dearly or forget you ever existed instead
In your search for forever, don't forget to be
mindful of words, actions and patterns.
These will truly tell you everything beyond what you may blindly
be hoping for while chasing a dream that may shatter.
Strangers once again

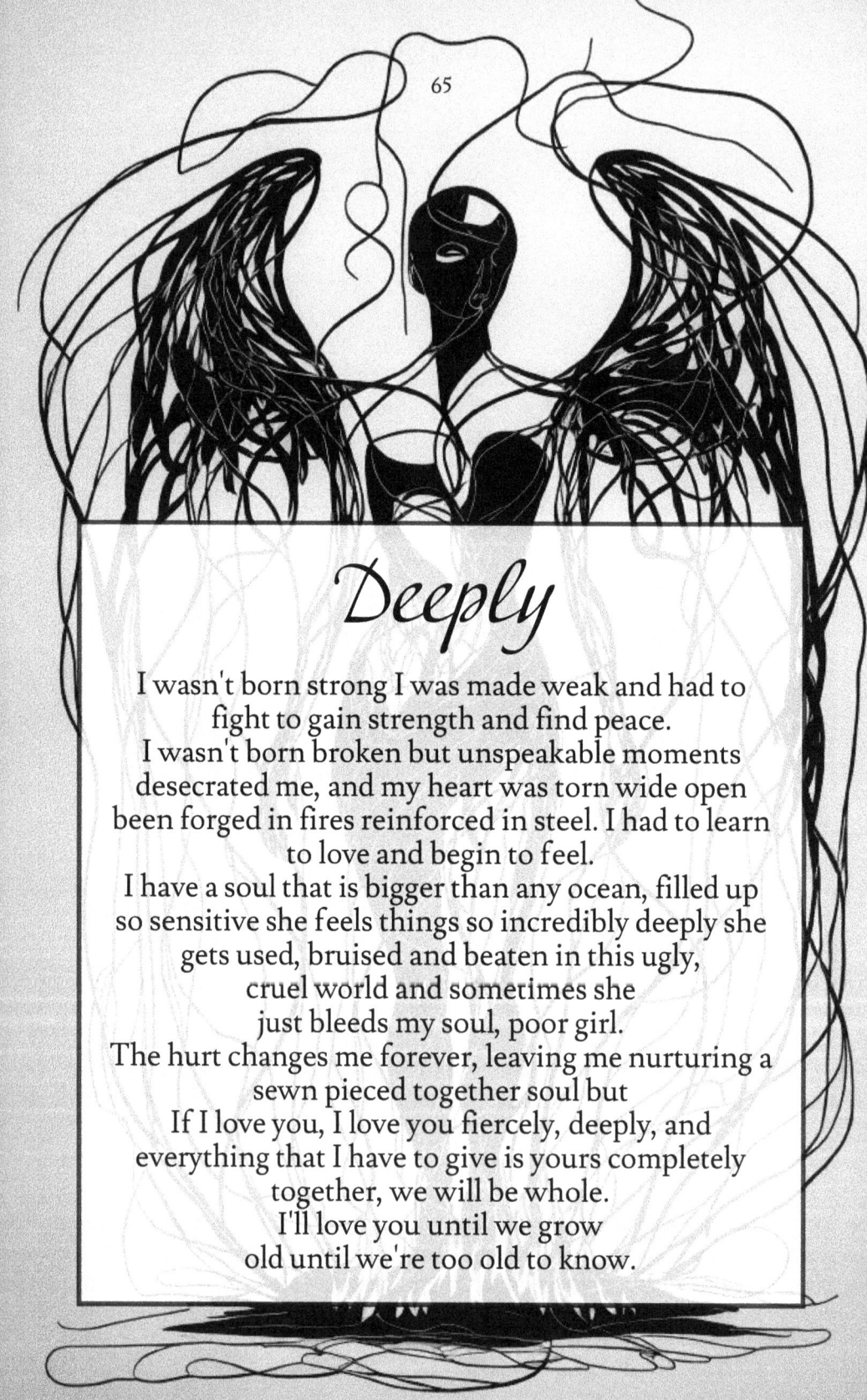

Deeply

I wasn't born strong I was made weak and had to
fight to gain strength and find peace.
I wasn't born broken but unspeakable moments
desecrated me, and my heart was torn wide open
been forged in fires reinforced in steel. I had to learn
to love and begin to feel.
I have a soul that is bigger than any ocean, filled up
so sensitive she feels things so incredibly deeply she
gets used, bruised and beaten in this ugly,
cruel world and sometimes she
just bleeds my soul, poor girl.
The hurt changes me forever, leaving me nurturing a
sewn pieced together soul but
If I love you, I love you fiercely, deeply, and
everything that I have to give is yours completely
together, we will be whole.
I'll love you until we grow
old until we're too old to know.

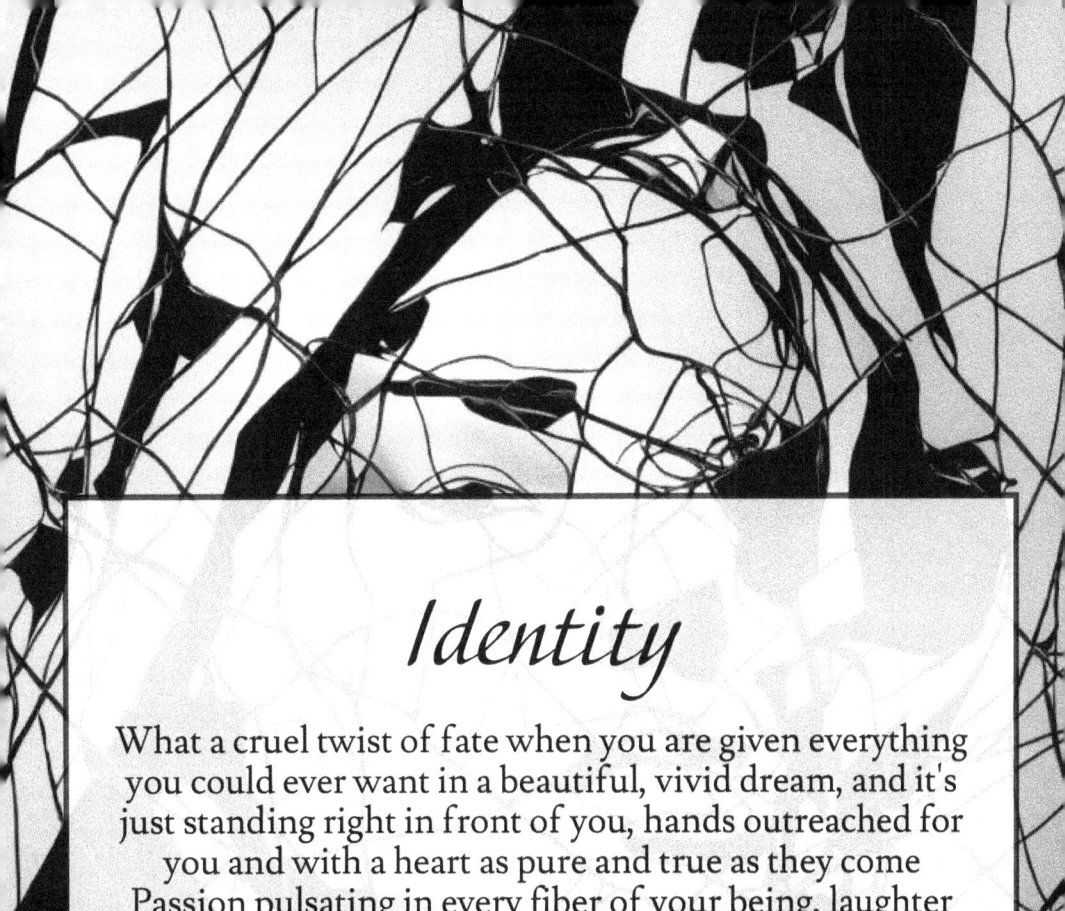

Identity

What a cruel twist of fate when you are given everything
you could ever want in a beautiful, vivid dream, and it's
just standing right in front of you, hands outreached for
you and with a heart as pure and true as they come
Passion pulsating in every fiber of your being, laughter
and friendship abundantly clear and all right there for the
taking, but now for the sad twist in the plot
Happily and free in your heart, you look in the mirror and
don't know who it is that you see looking back at you,
a victim of stolen identity.
Over years of time, other voices have taken over and
seeped into your head, taking turns convincing
you of who they want you to be instead.
Shaming you till you feel persuaded and weak with no
fortitude left you of your own helplessly
agree eager to please
pleasing everyone but yourself chains your soul
Deep inside your heart, it feels the truth and is sad and
disagrees, and you just wish and want nothing more than
to have your own voice own dream and to be left alone to
breathe and live happily free.

See me

Do you see what I hide
Can you see behind my olive eyes
Sometimes I think I see you there
It's hard to say, but I catch your stare
Are you feeling that certain one thing
Do you have the same sense I'm sensing
It's not really that I'm shy
And it's not really that I lie about my life
It's just it's my place that I feel safe inside
I don't care to share details, so don't pry
when I choose to elaborate, it makes me cry
Those who truly want you will search the
depths of your soul, turn over every stone to
their feelings will show
If I choose to show you
let you feel me truly see me
share with you my heart it means you are like
no other, so very special, and I will love you
completely until the day we part

Expectations

Expectations can be a double edged sword in a
world full of so many different wandering souls.
Because of who you are, you expect
to be given the same treatment in return.
Unfortunately, this is not always how
the story unfolds, and so you learn.
Learn to sit back and watch what
will be done in an effort towards you.
And not just listen to words that
are meant to confuse and fool you.
When you teach yourself and others how you
want to be treated, you start to reject anything
that is less than what you deserve and is needed.

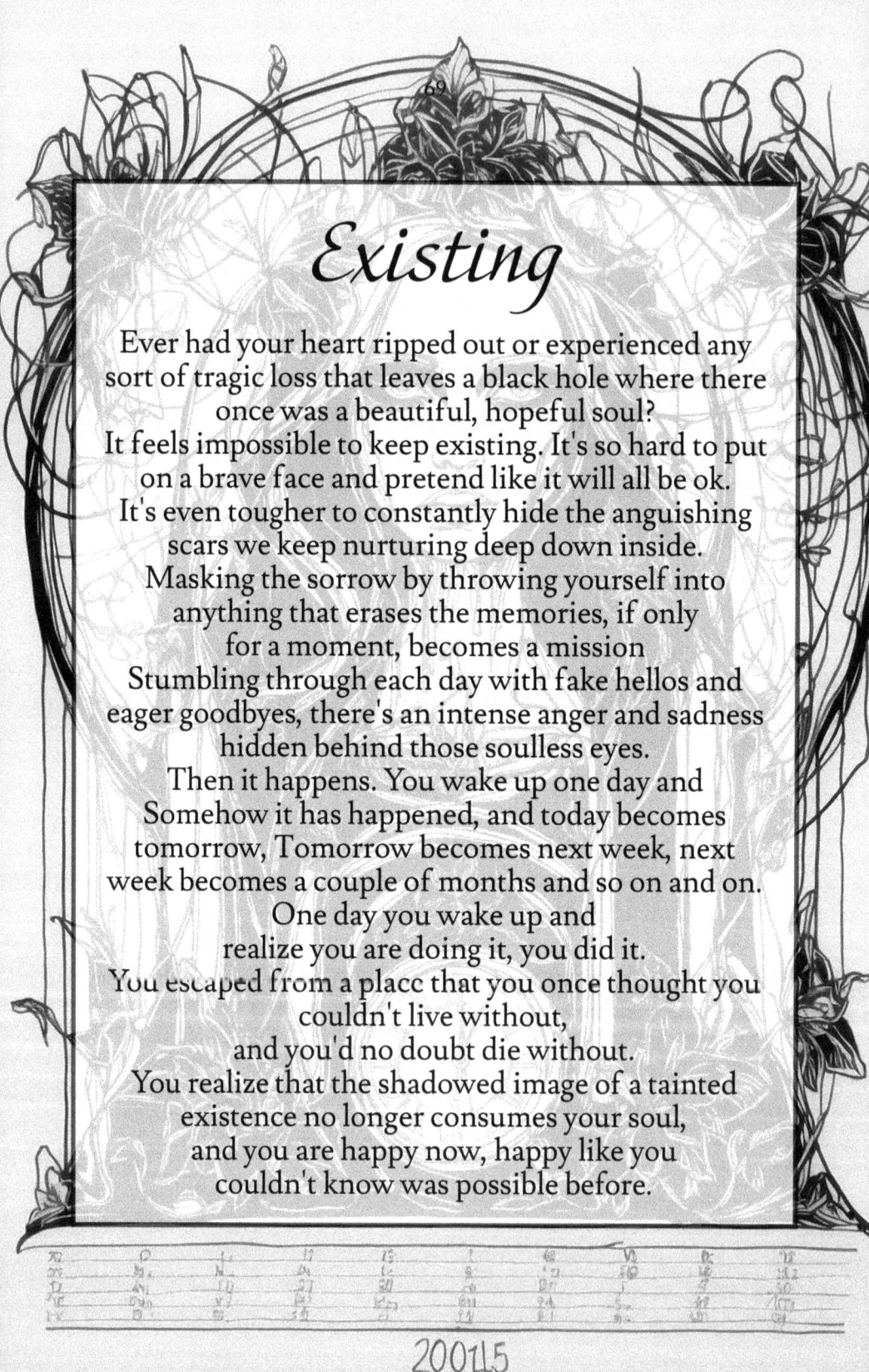

Existing

Ever had your heart ripped out or experienced any
sort of tragic loss that leaves a black hole where there
once was a beautiful, hopeful soul?
It feels impossible to keep existing. It's so hard to put
on a brave face and pretend like it will all be ok.
It's even tougher to constantly hide the anguishing
scars we keep nurturing deep down inside.
Masking the sorrow by throwing yourself into
anything that erases the memories, if only
for a moment, becomes a mission
Stumbling through each day with fake hellos and
eager goodbyes, there's an intense anger and sadness
hidden behind those soulless eyes.
Then it happens. You wake up one day and
Somehow it has happened, and today becomes
tomorrow, Tomorrow becomes next week, next
week becomes a couple of months and so on and on.
One day you wake up and
realize you are doing it, you did it.
You escaped from a place that you once thought you
couldn't live without,
and you'd no doubt die without.
You realize that the shadowed image of a tainted
existence no longer consumes your soul,
and you are happy now, happy like you
couldn't know was possible before.

Fate

Sometimes, I think it's been fate trying to trick me
throughout my life by presenting me with that one lesson
difficult to learn in many enticingly beautiful disguises.
Does fate possess such cruel
intentions the driving needs to be right
Or is she loyal and consistent, wanting only to fulfill my
wildest dreams and desires? Can I resist fate
when it's standing before me, staring me in the face
Will I learn the difference between the possibility of what
I hope for and what's actual reality, my fate
I suppose the only answer I can imagine
being true is if I am able to successfully resist you.
I believe you are, again, a mere test of my intelligence.
Oh, how I wish I could be wrong about being right
Oh, how I want more of you with all of my might
Only time will reveal if this is just
another game that fate plays with me
Or if I finally get it right and find
happily ever after so deservingly

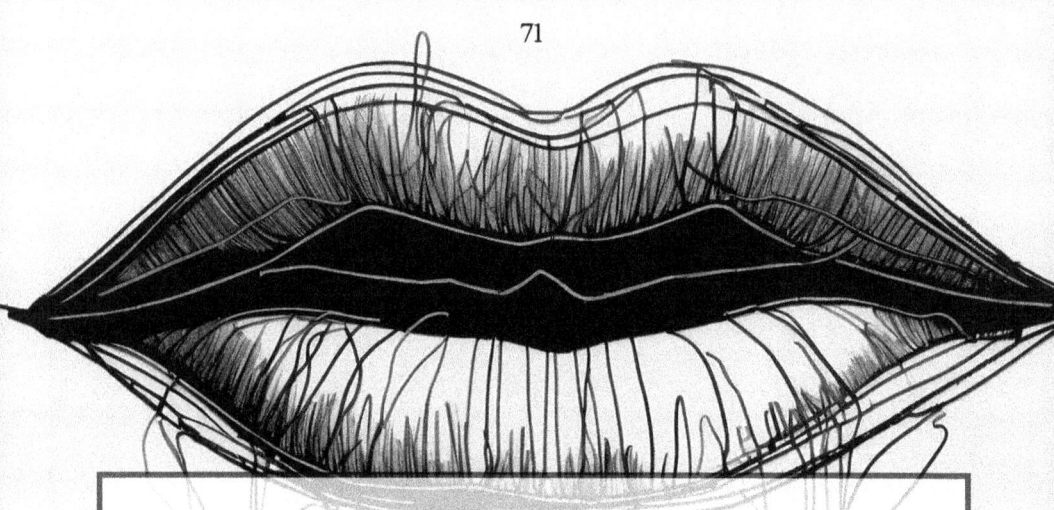

No words spoken

When no words are spoken, so much that
should've been said gets left unsaid.
Were those unspoken words the ones
that could've changed things maybe created
a different circumstance instead
Are they what kept what would've happened from
happening, and now you're left filled with regret
Maybe they could've offered peace
where now you feel incomplete in your head.
Could've offered valid justification
where doubt consumes and divides instead
When no words are spoken,
too many possibilities are left for fate to decide.
Speak all the words that are in your heart
that you feel and want to say.
Make it so there is nowhere for doubt to hide.
Say what you need to say and then
walk away feeling that you did everything you
could and one way or another, you will be fine.
In the end, it will all be ok.

Believing

Believing and following without ever questioning
ideology for years and through many
voices is called brainwashing or persuasion.
Belief while questioning, challenging and redefining
the outdated rules in order to obtain an acceptable
compromise of both what you want and what is expected
is a show of growth and intelligence.
Question everything, challenge all, seek within
your soul and accept your own truth.
Proud, Authentic and brutally honest

Tortured

Untie me
Release me
Unchain me
Don't tease me
Touch me
Caress me
Feel me
Please me
don't want you
Want me
Need me
Can't stop
Need you to go
Don't leave
You imprinted on my soul

Shamed

My body is not a temple.
It houses the deepest damaging scars.
My body brings me no joy,
and it allows me none from others.
I am not a toy.
It still fights through the pain
and hides away in eternal shame.
Where touching and pleasing others
might send them into sheer pleasure
I fight with all my might to fit in and just be alright with
whatever, enduring endless terrors.
You walk this world taking what's not yours.
Where is karma now when
she's needed to avenge my scars
Every day, I awaken and start out
into the world still broken but clinging to hope that there
may be one who possesses the magic to melt the
pieces of all my scars into one Frankenstein heart.
Once it's electrified to life, it will never feel hurt again,
and everything will forever be alright,
and this I wish for with all my might.
Because deep down, my soul still hides
glorious beauty inside, and she sings quietly

Lessons

And it is now when my words have been set into motion
and are followed by swift, silent action that you must
understand it is not that you are gone from my heart or
stricken from my soul but that my defenses have kicked
in, keeping me from softening, breaking down
my wholeness exposing my weakness.
Not letting you back in keeps me from falling prey to all
the pain I have worked so hard for years to banish.
My soul can't afford another steep price to pay. I know the
signs now when I see them, I know when to evoke
silence and when to walk away from temptation.
There was so much I wanted to say, and I wish so much
that I could've stayed, but I learned from my lessons
through the years and will continue on my journey,
laughing, singing and living life without learning any
more lessons or accumulating more tears.

Safe n Sound

Laying on the end of the bed, tears rolling and
horrific thoughts running through
my head, you stole my childhood.
You were supposed to keep me
safe and sound like family should
You broke the rules to make your demons happy.
There, where only those with permission
could go, you went uninvited and forbidden.
You took what was mine, and from that
moment on, I have never been fine.
Now you are gone, and the scars still remain,
but at least I can finally say good riddance.

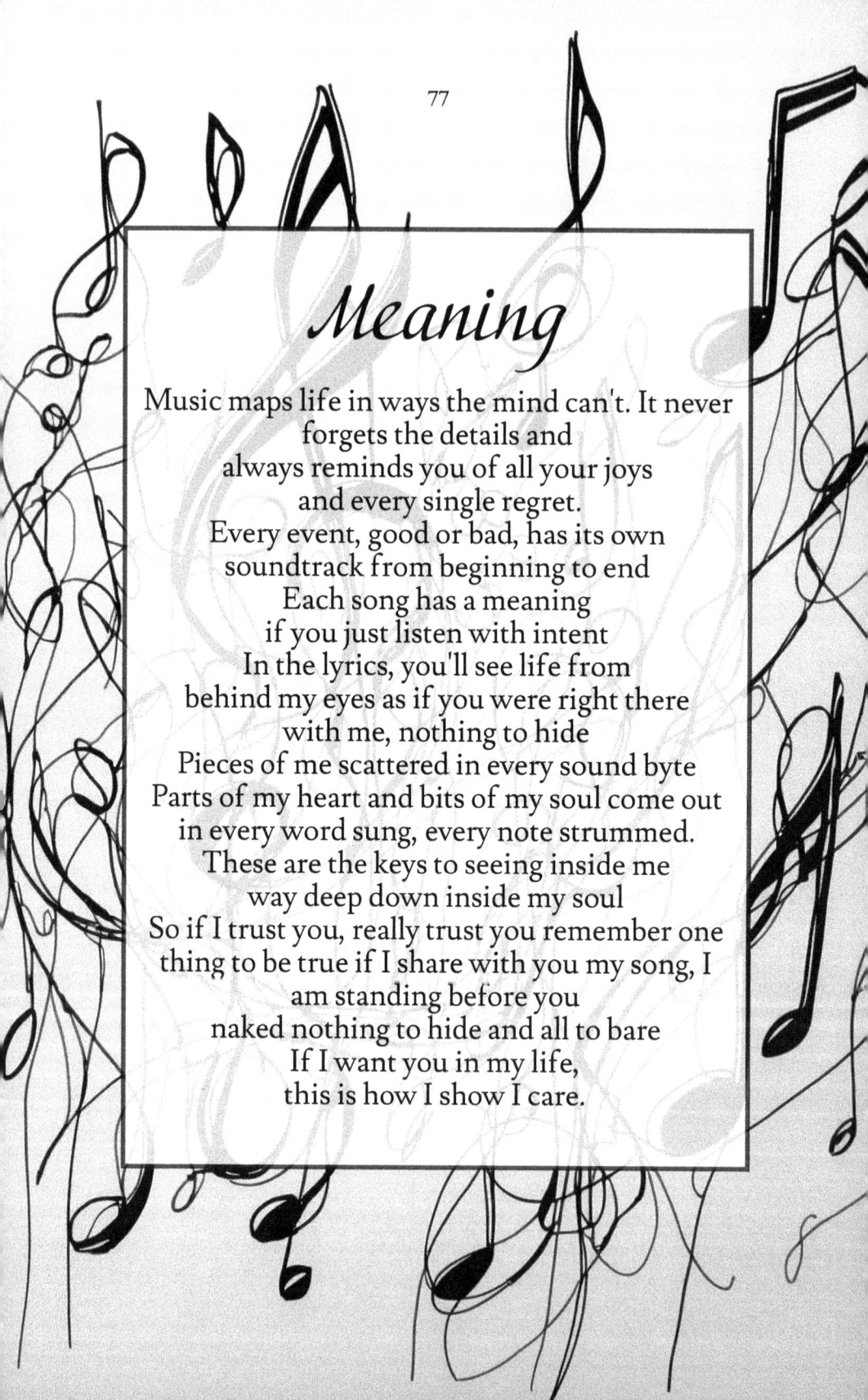

Meaning

Music maps life in ways the mind can't. It never
forgets the details and
always reminds you of all your joys
and every single regret.
Every event, good or bad, has its own
soundtrack from beginning to end
Each song has a meaning
if you just listen with intent
In the lyrics, you'll see life from
behind my eyes as if you were right there
with me, nothing to hide
Pieces of me scattered in every sound byte
Parts of my heart and bits of my soul come out
in every word sung, every note strummed.
These are the keys to seeing inside me
way deep down inside my soul
So if I trust you, really trust you remember one
thing to be true if I share with you my song, I
am standing before you
naked nothing to hide and all to bare
If I want you in my life,
this is how I show I care.

Beautiful Storm

There's thunder in her eyes
And lightening in her soul
The most beautiful storm
A gorgeous sight to behold
Her voice carries in the wind
Listen as she sings
Music ignites all throughout the night sky
Fills the air with most of everything
She strikes, illuminating wildly
Heavenly sent and beguiling
Hold her don't let her go
Because just like when a beautiful
storm passes through, it eventually ends
Wild and awe-inspiring still
There will only be traces of her left
behind in pictures, songs and memories
Captured in time

Our song

Days come and days go
Weeks and months they pass me by
Our song comes on, and I'm taken right back
to that special place in time.
To then, when laughter filled the air
To then, when our eyes would meet,
anyone standing near could feel our heated stare.
To a moment where there were lingering kisses
and hands wildly running in hair
Our song played in the background,
forging memories of every single moment.
Now, whenever I hear it play,
every time our song comes on,
it takes me back to my happy place
with you and that place in time.
Life goes on, but I still think
of you every time they play.
Our song

Hold on

Wanting so badly to hold on to you
But needing intently to set you loose
You have affected me in every single way
You have infected me and I can't seem to escape
Seems there is no quick cure for
what ails me but only the measure of time
My head knows logically that one day I'll be fine
But my soul just feels empty and still
holds onto the memory of your face
There's just too much between
us that time cannot erase
Wanting to hold on so badly
wanting my heart to win this time
I'll keep that memory of your
beautiful face in a safe and secret
place that only I can find

Daughter

Have you ever just looked at her with those golden sand
colored ringlet curls and eyes filled of the bluest skies
and thought that's my whole life standing right there?
That's my angel, my best friend
the biggest part of me... my daughter
The only one I'll ever truly love
The very best part of me

Tempting

Only those that have felt the
universe shift will understand this
But just a glance from wanting eyes paired with
a mischievously sideways smile can set your soul a blaze
causing you to lose yourself in every inappropriate way
A passing touch that electrifies you sets you
on course to fill your hearts every desire
Stolen moments linger in the steamy air
where passionate kisses entice illicit affairs
In the throws of undeniable chemistry are the only moments
that feel truly completely freeing and exciting
It is in these incredible fleeting moments
where your future late night dreams are made and
where your reality fades carelessly away
tempting moments persuade

Deception

You follow me surrounding me everywhere
Eyes fixed on listening to all my fears
There's never been another
to make it feel this way
Or at least that's what you've
worked so hard to make me say
Each string is meticulously attached
When the music plays, you sit back
Reveling in the show you orchestrated
Collector of souls and manipulator of lies
Maestro of puppets, ruiner of lives

Water

If you are looking for me look for me to be
where the nearby waters flow free
If there is an ocean at my feet you'll
find me riding the waves and walking its shores
pondering life on its bronze sandy beach
A relentless river flowing calls me to it's jagged edge where
I will wander it for hours sorting the thoughts in my head
Ponds and lakes beckon me to walk on in to retreat where
I'll drown my feelings under their waters so deep
With a mermaids heart drawn to waters serenity this is
where I always find internal peace and
visit with old memories that I secretly keep

They

They say everything in life happens for a reason?
Who are these they people anyway, and are they qualified
to make such vague and unapologetic conjectures?
Maybe they lie.
They could be aspiring demons from hell or county
prisoners on lockdown in the local jail.
Some things happen for specific reasons, and some
happen as a direct result of a lack of something needed.
But the worst things happen for reasons that do not
seemingly exist and are often unexplainable
where no logic or common sense exists.
These inexplicable things leave an empty void where
words could've easily been said instead, like goodbyes, I
love you, I am angry, why's and
why nots and please stays, let's try.
Actions could've stopped a motion from being set forth,
and actions could've caused one to deactivate and stop.
I guess it's all up to fate
tick tock

Wondering

I catch myself wondering what it would
be like to know your scent intimately.
How the sound of your
voice changes with every quiver and moan
I wanna know the smile that turns into
pleasure whenever I look up from your within
What your hair feels like on
my face and wrapped up in my hands
Will I still feel your touch
afterwards lingering on my skin
Will the taste of you send me sensually to heaven
I catch myself wondering, and it makes me grin

Patterns

I held you up on the highest platform
Became your muse and watched as you performed
Mental disturbance initiated your fall from grace
You almost got away
with it you are a fraudulent disgrace
A single thread bound tightly to a lie unraveled
meticulously curated patterns
Shameless maniacal, and manipulating plans
well on your way to having everyone fooled
Inflated ego, catch me if you can
Outdone by your own undoing
Your patterns served against you
and blew up in your face
Patterns don't lie or change easily be careful because
what you see you actually are seeing

You

I have looked for you in everything
and everywhere since that last day
There are so many things that I want to say
I'd make all your doubts and fears go away
But the only voice that carries
any weight right now is yours
The only person who can make this all it should be is you
I believe in you but you don't believe in yourself
I'd fight for you but I'd be the only one fighting
So staying silent is the only way
I know to help you but it destroys us
If you ever come calling it will only be because
your voice inside you became the loudest over them
all and nothing could stop you from making the call
The only one left to fight for and
believe in you is you because I already do
There will always be a place
that belongs only to you deep down Inside me
If you ever get your head on straight come find me
For now though I will
continue on my journey living silently
I am a choice not an option,
never someone's option

Picking memories

Out for a long evening stroll
On a quest to repair my spirit heal my soul
I came across our field from so long ago
I'm sure it's the same one with
all our memories we planted together
I knew to stay away just wanted to look for a
quick moment a moment turned hours into
time that I'd soon regret
There's even a sign I planted here to yielding me
to steer clear, and yet I cannot help myself
I begin picking the memories anyway
First, I find some with smiles and laughter, but
then they turn dark, bringing me to immediate
despair and displeasure
Get up off your knees your smarter than this
you learned your lesson,
and now you know better
Bandage that heart, dry those eyes
this will be our final goodbye
I'll burn this field right down to the ground
There's more to my life than the memories here
I am no longer bound to what I left behind
in our field of tortured souls and eternal lies
Is where that part of you and I will die

True

Being true to who I am means having
to lose you, even though I don't want to
You challenge my intuition
and make me question my senses
Your smile leaves me mystified and utterly defenseless
Knowing my weaknesses is a strength
learned through hard lessons, and from them,
these are my true confessions.

Acknowledgement:

Thank you, my angel, my mini best friend and to those who have brought my words and feelings to life again.

Thank you my hope.
CANCER SUCKS

***

About The Author

Born and raised in Florida but recently moved to be near my child. I, as many others have, had a hard life with many very hard, painful lessons to learn. As a young person in high school, I would listen to music and write to help me learn how to cope and express how I was feeling. Writings come from within, from what I feel to what I experienced and also what I feel from another person's feelings. I won a literary competition for a short story I wrote on child abuse, but after that, I started writing privately. My greatest accomplishment was raising the most amazing young woman, of whom I am so very proud.

***